Table of Contents

Fan's Dictionary – Aston Villa F.C. Songbook

About This Book 3
1-9 5
A 6
B 16
C 21
D 30
E 34
F 38
G 40
H 44
I 49
J 51
L 59
M 61
N 67
O 70
P 72
Q 81
R 83
S 84
T 92

U 107
V 108
W 111
Y 127

Over the years Aston Villa F.C. fans have created incredible atmospheres in football grounds and come up with some of the creative chants and songs. This book is a guide for these chants and songs written by the Aston Villa F.C. supporters. From the Paul McGrath My Lord, Holte Enders In The Sky, My Old Man, When You're Smiling, You Are My Villa, Villa Till I Die, to songs dedicated to the various players and staff, the very best of the terrace chants, songs, and timeless classics, this book will delight and entertain in equal measure and honors every single Aston Villa F.C. fan who has ever sung in support for the team throughout its proud history.

All the songs and chants in this book are written and sang by the Aston Villa F.C. supporters during football matches, at pubs and bars or posted to message boards, they are not the thoughts or views of the authors.

WRITE TO US

We greatly value your opinion. We would love to hear your thoughts and recommendations about this book so we can improve! Write to us: fansdictionary@gmail.com

COPYRIGHT

Copyright © 2020 by Fan's Dictionary

The author have provided this book to you for your personal use only. Thank you for buying and for complying with copyright laws by not reproducing, scanning, or distributing any part of it in any form without permission.

10 BRUMMIES IN THE PUB

There were 10 Bluenose b*stards in the pub,
There were 10 Bluenose b*stards in the pub,
There were 10 Bluenose b*stards,
10 Brummie b*stards in the pub.

And the Villa boys from Aston knocked one out,
And the Villa boys from Aston knocked one out,
The Villa boys from Aston,
The Villa boys from Aston knocked one out.

There were 9 Bluenose b*stards in the pub,
There were 9 Bluenose b*stards in the pub,
There were 9 Bluenose b*stards,
9 Brummie b*stards in the pub…

(Keeps going until no Bluenose b*stards are left in the pub)

10 DALMATIANS

10 dalmatians walking down the street,
And if Carson Young wants a bite to eat,
There'll be 9 dalmatians walking down the street.
9 dalmatians walking down the street,
And if Carson Young wants a bite to eat,
There'll be 8 dalmatians walking down the street.
8 dalmatians walking down the street,
And if Carson Young wants a bite to eat,
There'll be 7 dalmatians walking down the street.
7 dalmatians walking down the street,
And if Carson Young wants a bite to eat,
There'll be 6 dalmatians walking down the street.

(Keeps going until no dalmatians are left walking down the street)

A LITTLE BIT OF

A little bit of Milner in oir lives,
A little bit of Ashley down the sides,
A little bit of Petrovs what we need,
A little bit of Gabby with his speed,
A little bit of Collins in defense,
A little bit of Downing he immense,
A little bit of cheering from the fans,
Cause we're the best team in the land,
Na na na na na na na na na.

A TERRIBLE PLACE

I know a ground it's a terrible place,
They call it St. Andrews it's such a disgrace,
They've got air conditioning and that is the truth,
Cause I've been and I've seen the holes in the roof...

..Singin we hate o' we hate the city, we hate o' we hate the blues,
We hate o' we hate the city and we're quite content when they lose...

ADAMA TRAORE

Adama,
Adama,
Adama,
He's too good for Barça,
Barça,
Barça,
That's why he joined the Villa,
The Villa,
The Villa,
And that's the way he likes it,
He likes it,
he likes it,
Oooooo ooooohh,
Oooooo ooooohh.

ALL I CARE ABOUT

I don't care about Scouser's,
They don't care about me,
All I care about is AVFC...

ALLAN HUTDOG

The Scottish Cafu,
The Scottish Cafuuuuuuu,
Allan Hutton,
The Scottish Cafuuuu.

ALLEZ ALLEZ ALLEZ

Every week we follow,
The boys in claret and blue.
We've conquered all of Europe,
In 1982,
The Villa boys from Aston...

..We travel near and far,
You'll hear us singing,
From the stands of Villa Park.

Allez, Allez, Allez,
Allez, Allez, Allez,
Allez, Allez, Allez,
Allez, Allez, Allez...

AND IT'S ASTON VILLA

And it's Aston Villa,
Aston Villa FC,
We're by far the greatest team,
The world has ever seen...

ANDREAS WEIMANN

He scored a goal and the Holte went wild,
And I just can't seem to get enough of,
Dadadadadadadadadad Andreas Weimann.

ANDREAS WEIMANN 2

Du du du-du du-du,
Du du du-du du-du,
Du du du-du du-du,
Andi Weimann.

ANDY GRAY

Oh Andy, oh Andy,
Your the greatest the Holte End say,
Oh Andy, oh Andy,
We'll be with you all the way…

ANDY GRAY 2

He's here, he's there,
He's every f**kin where,
Andy gray,
Andy Gray.

ASHLEY YOUNG

Singing aye aye Ashley,
Ashley Young,
Singing aye aye Ashley,
Ashley Young,
Singing aye aye Ashley,
Ashley Young,
Aye aye Ashley, Ashley Young.

ASHLEY YOUNG 2

Ashley Young's magic,
He wears a magic hat,
And when he signed for Villa,
He said I fancy that,
He didn't sign for Birmingham,
Or Arsenal cause there sh**e,
He signed for Aston Villa cause we're fu**ing dynomite...

ASHLEY YOUNG 3

He plays down the left,
He plays down the right,
That boy Ashley Young,
Made City Look Sh*te...

ASHLEY YOUNG 4

Who's that running down the left wing and the right?
Is it shaun Wright Phillips? No hes s*ite!
It isn't Aaron Lennon, someone better tell em,
It's Ashley Young hes fucking Dynamite...

ASHLEY YOUNG 5

He's small, He's thin,
He runs down the wing
Ashley Young, Ashley Young.

ASTON VILLA HERE WE GO

Yippie yi aye yippie aye,
O Aston Villa,
Here we go.

ASTON ASTON VILLA

Aston, Aston Villa,
We are the boys in claret and blue,
Aston, Aston Villa we are the boys who know what to do,
We wear our colours with dignity,
For we have honour and history,
Aston, Aston Villa,
We are the boys who know what to do,
Aston, Aston Villa c'mon you lions,
We will follow you.

AXEL TUANZEBE

You see him playing football with his head and with his feet,
Everybody's dancin' to the Tuanzebe beat,
Tuanzebe and a Tuanzebe,
Tuanzebe,
Zebe,
Zebe,
Zebe...

BARRY BANNAN

Barry Bannan,
Da da da da,
Barry Bannan,
Da da da da,
Barry Bannan,
Da da da da...

BIRMINGHAM IS FULL OF FUN

Oh Birmingham,
(Oh Birmingham),
Is full of fun,
(Is full of fun),
Oh Birmingham is full of fun,
It's full of tits, f**ny and the Villa,
Oh Birmingham is full of fun...

BIRMINGHAM ARE YOU LISTENING

Birmingham, are you listening,
To the song that we're singing,
We're walking along,
Singing our song,
S***ting on the City as we goooooo...

BIRMINGHAM'S SMALLEST CLUB

One hundred years and won f*ck all,
Small Heath, Small Heath,
One hundred years and won f*ck all,
Small Heath, Small Heath,
They've changed their name,
They're still the same,
And now they're doing down again,
Small Heath Alliance,
Birmingham's smallest club.

BOOTS ARE MADE FOR KICKING

Boots are made for kicking,
Knives are made for stabbing,
And if you are a city fan I'll kick you f**ing heading,
Doo doo dooo dooo
Doo doo dooo dooo
Doo doo dooo dooo Villa.

BORING BORING ARSENAL

Boring Boring Arsenal,
Boring Boring Arsenal,
Are you Arsenal,
Are you Arsenal,
Are you Arsenal in disguise?

BRIAN LITTLE WALKS ON WATER

Brian Little walks on water , la, la, la, la, la, la,la,la,la.
Brian Little walks on water , la, la, la, la, la, la,la,la,la.
Brian Little walks on water , la, la, la, la, la, la,la,la,la.
Brian Little walks on water , la, la, la, la, la, la,la,la,la...

BUBBLES

You can stick your fu*kin bubbles up your a*se,
You can stick your fu*kin bubbles up your a*se,
You can stick your fu*kin bubbles,
You can stick your fu*kin bubbles,
You can stick your fu*kin bubbles up your a*se...

BUILD A BONFIRE

Build a bonfire,
Build a bonfire,
Put the Baggies on the top,
Put the noses in the middle,
And burn the f***ing lot...

BYE BYE BIRMINGHAM

Pardew has the number for the championship,
League one,
League one,
Bye bye Birmingham,
F**k off to league one.

CAN YOU HEAR THE CITY SING

Can you hear the City sing,
Can you hear the City sing,
Can you hear the City sing,
Cos i cant hear a f*****g thing...

CARLOS CUELLAR

He's 6 foot 2 with curly hair Cuellar Cuellar,
He's 6 foot 2 with curly hair Cuellar Cuellar,
He's 6 foot 2 with curly hair his teeth are,
F****d but we don't care,
Carlos Cuellar Villa's centre half.

CARLOS CUELLAR 2

Na na na na na na na na,
Na na na na na na na na,
With his goofy teeth and curly hair,
He played for Rangers we don't care,
Carlos Cuellar Villa centre half.

CARLOS CUELLAR 3

Na na na na na na na na,
Na na na na na na na na,
Olive skin and curly hair,
Cross the ball into the air,
Carlos Cuellar Famous Centre half.

CARLOS CUELLAR 4

Curly hair and goofy teeth cuellar, cuellar,
He will f**k your wife when your asleep,
Carlos Cuellar Villa's centre half.

C-CREW

The C-Crew, yes we are the C-Crew,
The C-Crew we never run away,
We'll stand and fight the boys in blue and white,
The C-Crew are fighting today.

CHEER UP ALAN SHEARER

Cheer up Alan Shearer,
Oh how does it feel,
To go, down like the Baggies,
With your s*it football team...

CHEERIO

Cheerio,
Cheerio,
Cheerio,
Cheerio...

CHIM CHIMINEY

Chim Chiminey,
Chim Chiminey,
Chim Chim Cheroo,
We are the Ba*tards in Claret and Blue.

CHRISTIAN BENTEKE

There was a striker,
A Belgian striker,
Called Christian Ben-tek-e,
There was a striker,
A Belgian striker,
Called Christian Ben-tek-e...

CHRISTIAN BENTEKE 2

Oh Christian Benteke,
Oh Christian Benteke,
Oh Christian Benteke...

CIRCUS IN THE TOWN

There is a circus in the town, in the town,
Alex McLiesh is a clown, is a clown,
And Karen Brady is a f**king,
Sssslllllllllaaaaaaaaaaaa,
Aaaaaaaaaaaaaaaaaaaaaaaa,
Aaaaaaaaaaaaaaaaaaaaaaaaagggggggg,
And the blues are going down going down...

CIRCUS IN THE TOWN 2

There's a circus in the town, in the town,
Stevie Bruce is the clown, is the clown,
And K**** B**** is a f***ing s**g,
And the Blues are going down, going down.

CIRCUS IN THE TOWN 3

There's a circus in the town, in the town,
Trevor Francis is a clown, is a clown.

CITY IS OURS

The city is ours,
The city is ours,
F*ck off Small Heath,
The city is ours.

CITY REJECT

City reject,
City reject,
Whoah,
Whoah...

CLARET AND BLUE ARMY

Claret and blue army,
Claret and blue army,
Claret and blue army,
Claret and blue army...

CLASS OF 81/82

Six Dennis Mortimers,
Fiiiiive Ken McNaughttttttt,
Four Allan Evans,
Three Colin Gibson,
Two Kenny Swain,
And a Jimmy Rimmer as our goalieeee.

COCKNEY SCUM

Cockney scum,
Get out of brum,
Cockney scum,
Get out of brum...

COME ON VILLA

Come on Villa,
Come on Villa,
Come on...

COME TO BIRMINGHAM

Come to Birmingham, you will see,
Ansells Brewery, M&B,
We don't drink Whisky and we don't drink Rum,
We are the Villa boys from Brum...

COME TO SEE THE VILLA

Come to see the Villa,
You've only come to see the Villa,
Come to see the Villa,
You've only come to see the Villa...

CONOR HOURIHANE

Conor Hourihane,
Du, du, du, du, du,
Conor Hourihane,
Du, du, du, du, du...

DANCE IF YOU LOVE THE VILLA

All dance,
If you love Villa,
All dance,
If you love Villa,
All dance,
If you love Villa...

DARREN BENT

He's big, he's black,
He's fast on the attack,
Darren Bent
Darren Bent.

DARREN BENT 2

Ole ole ole ole,
Darren bent bent bent...

DARREN BENT 3

Bent Bent wherever you may be,
Your so worth your transfer fee,
Took the money and sunderland paid,
But you score every game.

DARREN BENT 4

He gets the ball,
He scores a goal,
He celebrates in front of the Holte,
Darren Bent is Villa's 39.
Na na na na na na na,
Na na na na na na na,
He gets the ball,
He scores a goal,
He celebrates in front of the Holte,
Darren Bent is Villa's 39.

DODGY REFS

S**t refs,
We always get s**t refs,
We always get s**t refs,
We always get s**t refs...

DOWN WITH THE BAGGIES

You're going down with the Baggies,
Down with the Baggies,
You're going down with the Baggies,
Down with the Baggies!

DWIGHT YORKE

Start spreading the news,
He's playing today,
He's gonna score a goal again,
Dwight Yorke,
Dwight Yorke...

If he can, score from there,
He'll score from, anywhere,
It's up to you,
Dwight Yorke,
Dwight Yorkeeeeeee,
Du du du-du...

EARL BARRETT

Five foot eight,
Not much weight,
Earl Barrett is f**king great.

EMILE HESKEY

Go go go go go go go go go go go go go go,
Go go go go go go go go go go go go go go,
Heskeyyyyyyyy,
You are too good, at scoring goals,
We appreciate your input Heskey.

EMILE HESKEY 2

There's only one Emile Heskey,
Only one Emile Heskey,
He used to be s*ite,
But now he's alright,
Walking in a Heskey wonderland...

EMILE HESKEY 3

When I'm with you Heskey,
I go out of my head,
I just can't get enough,
I just can't get enough,
All the goals you score for me and all the assists you get,
I just can't get enough,
I just can't get enough.
We slip and slide as we fall in love and,
I just can't seem to get enough of,
Duh duh duh duh duh duh duh,
Duh duh duh duh duh duh duh,
Emile Heskey.

EMPTY SEATS

They're here, They're there,
They're f*ckin everywhere,
Empty seats, empty seats...

ENGERLAND

Engerland,
Engerland,
Engerland,
Engerland,
Engerland,
Engerland...

ERIC DJEMBA-DJEMBA

Djemba,
Djemba-Djemba,
Eric Djemba-Djemba..

FEED THE HARE AND HE WILL SCORE (MARLON HAREWOOD)

Feed the hare,
Feed the hare,
Feed the h and he will score,
Feed the hare and he will score...

FOOTBALL IN A LIBRARY

De de der,
Football in a library,
De de der,
Football in a library...

FOREVER AND EVER

Forever and ever,
We'll follow our team,
We're Aston Villa,
We rule supreme.

We'll never be mastered,
By you, by you blue nosed b*stards,
We'll keep the claret and blue flag flying high.

GABBY AGBONLAHOR

Gabby, Gabby, Gabby,
Gabby Agbonlahor,
He's fast as f*ck,
He's fast as f*ck...

GABBY AGBONLAHOR 2

Gabby Agbonlahor,
Gabby Agbonlahor,
Gabby Agbonlahor,
Gabby Agbonlahor...

GABBY AGBONLAHOR 3

Gabby, Gabby, Gabby,
Gabby Agbonlahor,
He's gonna score,
He's gonna score.

GABBY'S BOOTS ARE MADE FOR SCORING

Gabby's boots are made for scoring,
And that's just what they'll do,
Gabby's boots are made for scoring,
And they're gonna s**t all over you...

GARETH SOUTHGATE

Sit down Pinocchio,
Sit down Pinocchio,
Sit down Pinocchio,
Sit down Pinocchio...

GARY SHAW

Gary Shaw, Gary Shaw,
Gary Gary Shaw,
When he get's the ball he's bound to score,
Gary, Gary Shaw.

GARY SHAW 2

Gary Shaw,
Gary Shaw,
Once he scores one he'll score more.

GAVIN MCCANN

He tackles and he passes,
He wrestles and harasses,
He gets up peoples asses,
He's better than zidane.

Gavin McCann,
(Clap, Clap),
Gavin McCann,
(Clap, Clap),
Gavin McCann,
Gavin McCann,
Gavin McCann...

GET INTO 'EM

F*ck em up,
Get into em,
F*ck em up,
Get into em...

GLORY GLORY ASTON VILLA

My eyes have seen the glory of the villa win the cup,
Seven times we've won it, no one else can catch us up,
We are the boys in claret and blue we are the chosen few,
And the Villa go marching on,
Glory glory Aston Villa,
Glory glory Aston Villa,
Glory glory Aston Villa
And the villa go marching on on on...

HABIB BEYE

Sunday, Monday, Habib Beye,
Tuesday, Wednesday Habib Beye,
Thursday, Friday, Habib Beye,
Saturdaaaay, Habib Beyeeeee....

HAVE YOU WON THE EUROPEAN CUP

Have you won the European Cup,
The European Cup,
The European Cup...

Have you won the European Cup,
The European Cup,
The European Cup...

HELLO HELLO WE ARE THE VILLA BOYS

Hello, hello,
We are the Villa boys,
Hello hello,
We are the Villa boys,
And if you are a City fan surrender or you'll die,
Cos we all follow the Villa...

HEY HEY SCOUSER

Hey, hey Scouser,
Ew aah,
I wanna knowwowow,
Wheres my alloy rims,
And my DVD's,
And my washing machine,
And my plasma screen...

HIDING FROM THE VILLA

Blues come down,
Blues come down,
Blues come down together,
Twenty coaches and a train,
Hiding from the Villa.

HOLTE END AGGRO

Bertie Mee said to Bill Shankly,
Have you heard of the North Bank Highbury,
Shanks said no, I don't think so,
But I've heard of the Holte End agro.
La, la, la, la, la, la, la, la, la
We are the Villa boot boys!

HOLTE END ARMY

Fight, fight where ever you maybe,
We are the boys from the Holte army,
And we'll lead you all,
Whoever you maybe,
We'll lead you all to the Holte army...

HOLTE ENDERS

As I walked down to Villa Park one dark and dusty day,
I spied a poor old City fan running far away,
I said to that poor City fan, it looks like you must die,
'Cuz you have seen the glory of,
Holte Enders in the sky.

Yippeeh aye aaaayyyy,
Yippeeh aye ooohhhh,
Holte Enders in the sky...

...We chased him through the terraces, we chased him down the streets,
But little did that City fan know that death must be his fate,
'Cuz Villa fans rule Birmingham and city fans know why,
'Cuz they have seen the glory of,
Holte Enders in the sky.

Yippeeh aye aaaaahhhh,
Yippee aye oooohhhhh,
Holte Enders in the sky.

I WANNA GO HOME

I wanna go home,
I wanna go home,
Liverpool's a s*ithole,
I wanna go home...

IN THE LIVERPOOL SLUMS

In the Liverpool slums,
They look in the dustbins for something to eat,
They find a dead dog and they think its a treat,
In the Liverpool slums...

IRELAND IS SUPERMAN

Ireland is superman,
Ireland is superman,
Ireland is superman...

IS THIS A LIBRARY

Is this a library,
Is this a library,
Is this a library...

IT'S ALL GONE QUIET OVER THERE

And it's all gone quiet over there,
And it's all gone quiet over there,
And it's all gone quiet,
And it's all gone quiet,
All gone quiet over there.

And it's all gone quiet over there,
And it's all gone quiet over there,
And it's all gone quiet,
And it's all gone quiet,
All gone quiet over there.

JACK GREALISH

Super, super Jack,
Super, super Jack,
Super, super Jack..

JEAN MAKOUN

Jean Makoun Makoun,
He'll pass the ball 40 yards
He's big and he's f**kin' hard,
Jean Makoun Makoun.

JEAN MAKOUN 2

Jean Makoun Makoun,
He comes from Cameroon,
He's gonna score very soon,
Jean Makoun Makoun.

JOHN CAREW

John Carew, Carew,
He likes a lap-dance or two,
He might even pay for you,
John Carew, Carew...

JOHN CAREW 2

John Carew Carew,
He's bigger than me and you,
He's gonna score one or two,
John Carew Carew...

JOHN CAREW 3

John Carew Carew,
Is better than all of you,
He even makes Zigic need the loo.
Cus he is John Carew.

JOHN CAREW 4

He shoots he scores he's 6 feet 4,
John Carew, John Carew,
He's lean he's mean he turns f***ing green,
John Carew, John Carew...

JOHN CAREW 5

Chim Chiminey,
Chim Chiminey,
Chim Chim Cheroo,
Who needs Wayne Rooney when we've got Carew?

JOHN CAREW 6

John Carew Carew, he's gonna terrorise you,
John Carew Carew, he's got a big d*ck too,
John Carew Carew, Birmingham wished they had you John Carew Carew.

JOHN CAREW 7

I knew from the first time I saw Carew Carew,
He's gonna score a goal for us or two or two,
You'll always find him in a pub,
Or perving down the rocket club,
We all love big John, Villa's number 10.

Na na na na na na na na na,
Big John Big John,
Na na na na na na na na na,
Big John Big John.

He plays for the team the pride of brum,
He scored two goals against the scum,
We all love big John,
Villa's Number 10.

JOHN CAREW 8

His arm band proved he was a claret,
Carew Carew,
He said he was a Villain,
Carew Carew,
We bought the lad from northern France,
He heads the ball and scores again,
John Carew, he's from Norway.

JOHN MCGINN

We've ot McGinn,
Super John McGinn,
Just don't think you understand,
Steve Bruce's man,
He's better than Zidane,
We'ver got super John McGinn.

JOHN TERRY

Woah,
Terry's on Tinder
Woah,
He's messaging your sister,
Woah,
He always gets his end away,
1.2.3.4...

JOLEON LESCOTT

The Elephant Man,
The Elephant Maaaaannnn,
Jo-le-on Lescott,
Is The Elephant Man.

JORDAN AYEW

Here we have Jordan Ayew,
He will score more than a few.

JORES OKORE

Ooo-korrr-aaaar suuuuper-star,
Sent down from Heaven after Paul McGrath.

JUAN PABLO ANGEL

Juan Pablo Angel,
There's only Juan Pablo Angel,
Juan Pablo Angel,
There's only Juan Pablo Angel...

LET'S ALL HAVE A DISCO

Let's all have a disco,
Let's all have a disco,
Na na na na,
Na na na na.

LET'S GO MENTAL

Let's go f*cking mental,
Let's go f*cking mental,
La la la la,
La la la la...

LIAM RIDGWELL

Liam Ridgwell,
What a w****r, what a w****r,
Liam Ridgwell,
What a w****r, what a w****r.

LOFTY THE LION

Your just a fat ginger lion,
Fat ginger lion.

LONG TIME AGO IN BIRMINGHAM

Long time ago in Birmingham,
Eighteen Hundred and Seventy-four,
By the light of a gas lamp,
This famous club was born,
Hark now hear the Villa sing,
A club was born that day
Who's name will live for evermore,
Aston V I L L A...

LUIS SUAREZ

Your teeth are offside,
Your teeth are offside,
Luis Suarez your teeth are offside..

MARC ALLBRIGHTON

His name is Allbrighton he wears the claret and blue,
I just can't get enough,
I just can't get enough,
He's born in Tamworth he's Villa through and through,
I just can't get enough,
I just can't get enough.

Hell never leave us and he loves the Holte,
And I just can't get enough,
Dudududududdudududu,
Marc Allbrighton.

MARTIN LAURSEN

Der Der Der Der Martin Laursen,
Der Der Der Der Martin Laursen,
Der Der Der Der Martin Laursen…

MARTIN LAURSEN 2

There's only one Martin Laursen,
One Martin Laursen,
He plays at the back,
But he's great in attack,
Walking in a Laursen wonderland...

MARTIN LAURSEN 3

Who's that coming out of defence,
It's Martin Laursen,
It's Martin Laursen.

MARTIN O'NEILL

Martin O'Neill,
Martin O'Neill,
Martin O'Neill,
Martin O'Neill...

MARTIN O'NEILL 2

Martin O'Neill,
Martin O'Neill,
Martin O'Neill,
Martin O'Neill,

When I was young, I had a dream,
To watch the greatest football team,
So here I am, the dream is real,
With Randy Lerner and Martin O'Neill,

Martin O'Neill,
Martin O'Neill,
Martin O'Neill,
Martin O'Neill,

Martin O'Neill,
Martin O'Neill,
Martin O'Neill,
Martin O'Neill...

MARTIN O'NEILL'S BARMY ARMY

Martin O'Neill's barmy army, A.V.F.C.,
Martin O'Neill's barmy army, A.V.F.C.,
Martin O'Neill's barmy army, A.V.F.C.,
Martin O'Neill's barmy army, A.V.F.C...

MARTIN O'NEILLS'S CLARET AND BLUE ARMY

Martin O'Neill's Claret and blue army,
Martin O'Neill's Claret and blue army,
Martin O'Neill's Claret and blue army,
Martin O'Neill's Claret and blue army...

MOUSTAPHA SALIFOU

Sali,
Salifou,
Sali,
Salifou...

MOUSTAPHA SALIFOU 2

Sali-Salifou,
Sali-Salifou,
Bullet bullet proof,
Sali-Salifou,
Sali-Salifou.

MY GARDEN SHED

My garden shed,
(My garden shed),
Is bigger than this,
(Is bigger than this),
My garden shed is bigger than this,
It's got a door, and a window,
My garden shed is bigger this...

MY HAMSTER'S CAGE

My Hamster's Cage,
(My Hamster's cage),
Is bigger than this,
(Is bigger than this),
My Hamster's cage is bigger than this,
It's got some straw and a spinning wheel,
My hamsters cage is bigger than this.

MY OLD MAN

My old man said 'be a city fan',
And I said' b***ocks you're a c**t (you're a c**t),
We hate the blues and we're gonna show it,
We hate the blues and we f**king know it,
With Spinksy and Burchy Alan Mcanally,
They're the boys who gonna do us fine,
You support the blues ur a blue nose b***ard and you ain't no friend of mine...

NATHAN BAKER

Ohh Nathan Baker is magic,
He wears a magic hat,
And if you threw a brick at him,
He would head the f*cker back,
Chester is his partner and he would do the same,
And when we get promoted we'll sing this song again...

NATHAN DELFOUNESO

Nathan Delfouneso,
Nathan Delfouneso,
Running down the wing,
See his Dreadlocks swing,
Nathan Delfouneso...

NEVER BEAT THE VILLA

Blues go down,
Blues do down,
Blues go down forever,
Come back up,
Will they f*ck,
Never beat the Villa...

NICE ONE SHEARER

Nice one Shearer,
Nice one son,
Nice one Shearer,
Now back to channel one!

NIGEL REO-COKER

De, de, der Nigel Reo-Coker,
De, de, der Nigel Reo-Coker,
De, de, der Nigel Reo-Coker...

NIGEL REO-COKER 2

Let's All do the Conga,
With Nigel Reo-coker,
Da, Da, Da, Da..
Da, Da, Da, Da.

NIGEL REO-COKER 3

You're just a short Paul Ince,
You're just a short Paul Ince.

NIGEL SPINK

Nigel Spink, rolls the ball to Platty,
He moves it onto Paul McGrath and onto Tony Daly,
Tony Daly down the wing like a torpedo,
Puts the ball up in the,
Aiiiiiiiiiiiiiiiiiiiiiiiiiiiiiiiiiiiiiiiiiiiiiiiiir...
For Tony Cascarino...

OH ST. ANDREWS

Oh St. Andrews,
(Oh St. Andrews),
Is full of sh*t,
(Is full of sh*t),
Oh St. Andrews is full of sh*t, full of sh*t,
Sh*t and more sh*t,
Oh St. Andrews is full of sh*t.

Oh Molineux,
(Oh Molineux),
Is full of sh*t,
(Is full of sh*t),
Oh Molineux is full of sh*t, full of sh*t, sh*t and more sh*t,
Oh Molineux is full of sh*t...

...Oh the hawthorns,
(Oh the hawthorns),
Is full of sh*t,
(Is full of sh*t),
Oh the hawthorns is full of sh*t, full of sh*t,
sh*t and more sh*t,
Oh the hawthorns is full of sh*t...

OLOF MELLBERG

Mellberg,
There's only one Mellberg,
There's only one Mellberg,
There's only one Mellberg...

ONE SONG

One song,
You've only got one song,
You've only got one song,
You've only got one song.

PAUL MCGRATH

He's the greatest defender in the whole wide world,
He's the man we call the Black pearl,
No one can beat him he's a one man wall,
You can always depend on our Paul,
Say oh ah Paul McGrath oh ah Paul McGrath.

PAUL MCGRATH MY LORD

Paul McGrath my lord, Paul McGrath,
Paul McGrath my lord, Paul McGrath,
Paul McGrath my lord, Paul McGrath,
Oh Lord Paul McGrath...

On the p*ss my lord, on the p*ss,
On the p*ss my lord, on the p*ss,
On the p*ss my lord, on the p*ss,
Oh Lord on the p*ss...

...It's your round my lord, it's your round,
It's your round my lord, it's your round,
It's your round my lord, it's your round,
Oh Lord it's your round...

PAUL MCGRATH MY LORD 2

Paul McGrath my lord, Paul McGrath,
Paul McGrath my lord, Paul McGrath,
Paul McGrath my lord, Paul McGrath,
Oh Lord Paul McGrath...

On the p*ss my lord, on the p*ss,
On the p*ss my lord, on the p*ss,
On the p*ss my lord, on the p*ss,
Oh Lord on the p*ss...

It's your round my lord, it's your round,
It's your round my lord, it's your round,
It's your round my lord, it's your round,
Oh Lord it's your round...

...On the p*ss my lord, on the p*ss,
On the p*ss my lord, on the p*ss,
On the p*ss my lord, on the p*ss,
Oh Lord on the p*ss...

S*it support my lord, s*it support,
S*it support my lord, s*it support,
S*it support my lord, s*it support,
Oh lord, s*it support...

Going down my lord, going down,
Going down my lord, going down,
Going down my lord, going down,
oh lord, going down...

Empty seats my lord, empty seats,
Empty seats my lord, empty seats,
Empty seats my lord, empty seats,
Oh lord, empty seats...

PAUL MCGRATH MY LORD 3

Paul McGrath my lord, Paul McGrath,
Paul McGrath my lord, Paul McGrath,
Paul McGrath my lord, Paul McGrath,
Oh Lord Paul McGrath...

On the p*ss my lord, on the p*ss,
On the p*ss my lord, on the p*ss,
On the p*ss my lord, on the p*ss,
Oh Lord on the p*ss...

It's your round my lord, it's your round,
It's your round my lord, it's your round,
It's your round my lord, it's your round,
Oh Lord it's your round...

S*it support my lord, s*it support,
S*it support my lord, s*it support,
S*it support my lord, s*it support,
Oh lord, s*it support...

...On the dole my lord, on the dole,
On the dole my lord, on the dole,
On the dole my lord, on the dole,
oh lord, on the dole...

PAUL MCGRATH (WE HAVE A FRIEND IN GOD)

Yes we have a friend in Jesus,
Yes we have a friend in God,
Yes we have a friend in Jesus,
And his name is Paul McGrath, Paul McGrath...

PETER WITHE

Hark now hear the Holte End sing a new kings born today,
His name is Peter Withe and he's better than Andy Gray!

PLAY FOR A BIG CLUB

Play for a big club,
You used to play for a big club,
Play for a big club,
You used to play for a big club...

POOR LITTLE COCKNEY

He's only a poor Cockney b**tard,
His face is all tattered and torn,
He made me fell sick so I hit him with a brick,
And now he don't sing anymore...

PRETTY BOTTLES IN THE AIR

I'm forever throwing bottles,
Pretty bottles in the air,
They fly so high and reach the sky,
And just like west ham they fade and die,
Tottenhams always running,
Arsenals running too,
I'm forever throwing bottles,
Pretty bottles in the air.

Villa,
(Clap, clap, clap),
Villa,
Villa.

PRIDE OF THE MIDLANDS, THE LIONS OF BRUM

We are the pride of the Midlands,
The lions of Brum,
We hate Small Heath, the Wolves and West Brom,
Coventry City on their way down,
And we will be there when the Villa are in Town...

PRIDE OF THE MIDLANDS, COCK OF THE NORTH

We are the pride of the Midlands, the cock of the north,
We hate all the Scousers and Cockneys of course.
We are the Villa and we are the best,
We are the Villa so f*ck all the rest...

...F*ck 'em all,
F*ck 'em all,
West Ham, Chelsea and Millwall,
'Cause we won't be mastered by no Cockney b*stards.

So score Villa score,
Villa score,
Villa score,
Villa score,
Once we've got one we'll get more.

So sing us an assembly when we get to Wembley,
Score, Villa score.

QUE SERA SERA

Que sera sera,
Wherever we be we be,
Goodbye Birmingham City,
Que sera sera.

RICHARD DUNNE

Dunne Dunne Dunne Dunne,
Dunne Dunne Dunne…

RUDY GESTEDE

Let it never be said that goal scoring is dead,
Because up front for Villa,
We've got Rudy Gestede,
With his big crazy hair,
He is class in the air,
He leaps like a salmon,
Jump with him if you dddddddddare.
Rudy, Rudy, Rudy,
Ruuud-dy,
Aaahhhhaaahhhhahhhhhhahhhh.

SAME OLD SCOUSER'S

Same Old Scouser's,
Always cheating...

SAMMY MORGAN

Six foot two, eyes of blue,
Sammy Morgan's after you,
La la la la, la la la, la laaaaar.

SAVO MILOSEVIC

Boom,
Boom,
Boom,
Let me hear you say Savo,
Savooooooooooooooo.

SEASIDE

Oh I do like to be beside the seaside,
Oh I do like to be beside the sea,
Oh I do like to be beside the prom, prom, prom,
Where the brass band plays,
F*ck off West Brom,
And Birmingham,
F*ck off West Brom,
And Birmingham....

SHALL WE SING A SONG FOR YOU

Shall we sing a,
Shall we sing a,
Shall we sing a song for you,
Shall we sing a song for you...

SHE WORE A CLARET RIBBON

She wore, she wore, she wore a claret ribbon,
She wore it for the Villa, in the merry month of May,
And when I asked, her why she wore that ribbon,
She said it's for the Villa, coz we're going to Wembley,Wembley, Wembley,
And we're the famous Aston Villa and we're going to Wembley,
Wembley, Wembley.

S*ITTING ON THE CITY AS WE GO

Walking along, singing a song,
Shitting on the city as we go, wooooaaah,
We own Birmingham,
You own Fergies used Gum,
Walking along, singing a song,
S*itting on the City as we go, wooooaaahh.

SHOES OFF, IF YOU LOVE VILLA

Shoes off, if you love Villa,
Shoes off, if you love Villa,
Shoes off, if you love Villa,
Shoes off, if you love Villa.

SIGN ON

Sign on,
Sign on,
With a pen in your hand,
And you'll never work again,
You'll never work again...

STAN COLLYMORE

Ohhhhhhhh,
Stany, Stanny, Stany, Stany, Stany
Collymoreeeeeeee.

STAND UP IF YOU LOVE VILLA

Stand up if you love Villa,
Stand up if you love Villa,
Stand up if you love Villa,
Stand up if you love Villa.

STAND UP IF YOU'VE GOT A JOB

Stand up if you've got a job,
Stand up if you've got a job,
Stand up if you've got a job,
Stand up if you've got a job...

STEPS OF THE HOLTE END

As I walked onto the steps of the Holte End,
As I walked onto the Holte End one day,
I spied a poor blues fan all cut up to ribbons...

...All cut up to ribbons and sh*t on they say,
I said to this blues fan what have they done to you,
And why have they treated you in such a way,
He said all I did sir was go up the Holte End,
And say Aston Villa were old men of clay,
The Holte did not like it they rose up above him they kicked in his b**locks,
They kicked in his head and now that poor blues fan is pushing up daisies,
He's pushing up daisies he's stone f**king dead,
Let this be a lesson to all of you blues fans who come up the Holte end to sing,
And to pray if you say just one word against Aston villa,
That will be the last word that you ever say,
We're the Villa, we're the Villa, we are the champions.

STEVE BRUCE

Stevie Bruce has got a big fat head,
He's got a big fat head, he's got a big fat head,
Stevie Bruce has got a big fat head,
He's got a big fat head, he's got a big fat head...

STEVE STONE

Stevie, Stevie Stone,
He's got no hair but we don't care,
Stevie, Stevie Stone.

STEVEN DAVIS

Steven Davis woooaaaah,
Steven Davis woooaaaah,
He plays next to McCann,
He's better than Zidane...

STEWART DOWNING

Stewart Downing,
Running down the wing,
Here the Holte end sing,
Stewart Downing.

STICK YER CAMERA

You can stick your f*cking camera up your a*se,
You can stick your f*cking camera up your a*se,
You can stick your f*cking camera,
Stick your f*cking camera,
Stick your f*cking camera up your a*se...

SUPER KEV MCDONALD

Super, super Kev, Super, super Kev,
Super, super Kev, Super Kev McDonald...

TESCO CARRIER BAGS

Always sh*t on the Tesco carrier bags,
Du du, du du du, du du.

THE BELLS ARE RINGING FOR THE ROYAL CLARET & BLUE

The bells are ringing for the claret and blue,
The fans are singing for the claret and blue,
Everybody is knowing, to the Villa they're going,
Where the Villa are showing,
We're the best in the land. Best in the land,
We're congregating for the claret and blue,
The Holte End's waiting for the claret and blue,
Everybody is knowing, to the Villa they're going,
Where the Villa are showing,
We're the best in the land. Best in the land.

THE BLUES ARE GOING UP

The Blues are going up,
And the Blues are going down,
The Blues are going down,
The Blues are going down.

The Blues are going up,
And the Blues are going down,
The Blues are going down,
The Blues are going down.

They're going up,
They're going down,
They're going up,
They're going down.

THE CITY

Sh*t on the City,
Sh*t on the City tonight,
(Ooo arr),
Sh*t on the City,
Sh*t on the City tonight,
Sh*t on the City,
Sh*t on the City tonight,
Everybody sh*t on the City,
Cos they're a load of Sh*te...

THE CITY IS OURS

The city is ours,
The city is ours,
Down with the hammers,
The city is ours.

THE FAMOUS HOLTE END

We are the famous,
The famous Holte End,
Clap clap clap-clap.

We are the famous,
The famous Holte End,
Clap clap clap-clap...

THE FIELDS OF TRINITY ROAD

As I stood outside the Holte-End steps,
I could hear a Holte-Ender calling,
Barton they have taken you away,
But before you went to heaven,
You left a great eleven,
Now there's glory,
Round the fields of Trinity Road...

THE LADS OF THE HOLTE ARMY

Fight, fight, whoever you may be,
We are the lads of the Holte Army,
And we'll beat you all,
Whoever you may be,
We are the lads of the Holte Army...

THE REFEREE

The referee's a w*nker,
The referee's a w*nker,
The referee's a w*nker...

THE SH*T ARE GOING DOWN

The s*it are going down,
The s*it are going down,
And now you are going to believe us,
And now you are going to believe us,
The s*it are going down.

THE VILLA IN CLARET AND BLUE

They play in blue and white,
The city are s**te, you know its true,
The villa in claret and blue,
Wooooaaaah,
Wooooahhhhhh.

THE VILLA IS OURS

The villa is ours,
The villa is ours,
F**k off back too small heath,
The villa is ours.

THE VILLA IS OURS 2

The villa is ours,
The villa is ours,
F**k off houllier,
The villa is ours.

THERE IS A TEAM IN BLUE AND WHITE

There is a team in blue and white,
They say that they are from brum,
They got knocked out of the FA Cup by Alec Stock's Fulham,
It was in the final minute the referee blew up,
And now them blue and white b**tards are out the FA Cup,
Ha ha ha ha ha ha ha ha ha ha ha...

THEY'RE COMING UP THEY'RE GOING DOWN

They're coming up, they're going down,
They're coming up, they're going down,
They're coming up, they're going down,
They're coming up, they're going down...

...Blues are coming up, but they're going straight back down,
They're going straight back down,
They're going straight back down,

Blues are coming up, but they're going straight back down,
They're going straight back down,
They're going straight back down,

They're coming up, they're going down,
They're coming up, they're going down,
They're coming up, they're going down,
They're coming up, they're going down,

Blues are coming up, but they're going straight back down...

THEY'RE S**T

They're s**t,
They're c**p,
They're never coming back,
Birmingham, Birmingham!

THOSE WERE THE DAYS

Those were the days my friend,
We took the Stretford End,
We took the Kop,
We took the f**kin lot,

We'd fight and never lose,
We f**kin hate the blues,
For we're the Villa,
The mighty claret and blues.

TOMMY JOHNSON

Super, super, Tom,
Super, super Tom,
Super, super Tom,
Super Tommy Johnson.

TOMMY SORENSEN

Woah Tommy Tommy,
Tommy, Tommy, Tommy, Tommy,
Sørensen...

TONY XIA

Dr. Tony went to Rome,
In a Ford Mondeo,
Brought us back a manager,
Roberto Di Matteo...

...Dr. Tony went to Bournemouth,
In a Skylark Buick,
Bought us back our leading man,
Oh Tommy Elphick.

Dr. Tony went to Verona,
In his Lamborghini,
Bought us back a goalkeeper,
Pierluigi Gollini.

Dr. Tony went to Reading,
In his brand new Roller,
Bought us back a midfielder,
Aaron Tshibola.

Dr. Tony went to Fulham,
In his Audi Sportback,
Bought us back the lethal striker,
Ross McCormack...

...Dr. Tony went to West Brom,
In a Ford Fiesta,
Bought us back a centre half,
Oh Jimmy Chester.

Dr. Tony returned to London,
In his new Cadillac,
Bought us back a defensive mid,
Oh Mile Jedinak...

TREVOR FRANCIS

Oh Oh Ohhh Francis,
Oh Oh Ohhh Francis,
I'd walk a mile and a bit,
To rub your face in some sh*t,
Oh Francis...

TREVOR FRANCIS 2

Cheer up Trevor Francis,
Oh what can it mean,
To a sad blue-nosed b**tard,
At a... sh*t football teammmm!

TYRONE MINGS

He joined us in the championship,
On loan,
On loan,
He joined us in the preimer leauge,
Tyrone,
Tyrone,
He's 6ft 5 he's in the air,
He's here he's there he's every where,
Tryone Mings he's villas centre half,
Na na na na na nana na.

TYRONE MINGS 2

He's here,
He's there,
He's every f*****g where,
Tyrone Mings,
Tyrone Mings.

USELESS

De, de, de, de,
F*cking useless,
De, de, de, de,
F*cking useless,
De, de, de, de,
F*cking useless,
De, de, de, de,
F*cking useless...

VILLA CLAP

Clap, clap, clap, cap, clap,
Villa,
Clap, clap, clap, cap, clap,
Villa,
Clap, clap, clap, cap, clap,
Villa,
Clap, clap, clap, cap, clap
Villa...

VILLA BOYS

Villa Boys we are here,
Wooa, wooa
Villa boys we are here,
S*ag your women and drink your beer...

VILLA FAN

When I was young my father said, son I have something to say,
Son you be a Villa fan, until your dying day,
He said son you be a Villa fan,
And that's the way to stay,
Happy to be a Villa fan until your dying day...

VILLA FOUR

Arsenal,
Chelsea,
Man Utd,
Liverpool,
F**k off cause here come the Villa,
Villa Villa Villa,
Villa Villa Villa,
Villa Villa Villa.

VILLA TILL I DIE

Villa till I die,
I'm Villa till I die,
I know I am I'm sure I am,
I'm Villa till I die.

WE ALL HATE BLUE SCUM

We all hate Blue scum,
We all hate Blue scum,
We all hate Blue scum,
We all hate Blue scum...

WE ARE THE BOYS IN CLARET AND BLUE

Allo allo, how do you do,
We are the boys in claret and blue,
We love to sing and we love to fight,
We hate the bastards in blue and white,
We'll sing this song of victory,
When we win division 3,
And the blues fan will never mock,
When they remember Bruce Rioch...

WE ARE THE CLARET AND BLUE ARMY

We are the claret and blue army,
We're all going to wembely,
We're going to lift the playoff cup when
Brucey takes us up,
Because Villa is the greatest football team.

WE ARE THE KINGS OF THIS CITY

Sing then where ever you may be,
We are the kings of this city,
And we'll lead you all,
Wherever you may be,
And we'll lead you allll,
to AVFC,

Villa, Villa, Villa.

WE BEAT THE SCUM 5-1

5-1,
We beat the scum 5-1,
We beat the scum 5-1,
We beat the scum 5-1...

WE FORGOT THAT YOU WERE HERE

We forgot,
We forgot,
We forgot that you were here,
We forgot that you were here...

WE HATE ALBION

We hate Albion,
Cuz we hate Albion,
We hate Albion,
Cuz we hate Albion...

WE HATE CITY

We hate city, we hate city, we hate city, we hate city, we are the city haters,
We hate city,
We hate city,
We hate city.

WE HATE THE CITY

Some say that St. Andrew's is a wonderful place,
I've been there myself it's a f*ckin' disgrace,
They say they have showers but we know the truth,
There's a hole in the roof where the rain p*sses through,
Singin' we hate, oh we hate the City, we hate the, we hate the blues,
We hate the, we hate the City, and we love it when the b*stards lose...

...They stand on the Tilton, they scream and they shout,
They shout about things they know f*ck all about,
They were owned by the Kumars,
Now they're owned by a pr*ck,
They play in those colours that make me feel sick,
Singin' we hate, oh we hate the city, we hate the, we hate the blues,
We hate the, we hate the City, and we love it when the b*stards lose.

They say that Trevor Francis was good on the ball,
But just like the rest of 'em, he won f*ck all,
They say that Karren Brady did a wonderful job,
But only with Sullivan's d*ck in her gob...

...Singin' we hate, oh we hate the city, we hate the, we hate the blues,
We hate the, we hate the City, and we love it when the b*stards lose.

WE PAY YOUR BENEFITS

We pay your benefits,
We pay your benefits,
We pay your benefits...

WE SHALL NOT BE MOVED

We shall not,
We shall not be moved,
We shall not,
We shall not be moved,
We're the pride of Birmingham,
We shall not be moved...

WE WANT OUR BALL BACK

We want our ball back,
We want our ball back,
We want our ball back,
We want our ball back...

WE WANT OUR RODNEY BACK

We want our Rodney back,
We want our Rodney back,
We want our Rodney back,
We want our Rodney back...

WE'LL SUPPORT YOU EVER MORE

Aston Villa,
Aston Villa,
We'll support you ever more,
We'll support you ever more...

WE'LL MEET AGAIN

We'll meet again,
Don't know where,
Don't know when,
But I know we'll meet again some sunny day!

WE'LL NEVER DIE

We'll never die,
We'll never die,
We'll never die,
We'll keep the Villa flag flying high,
And Aston Villa will never die.

WE'LL SING ON OUR OWN

We'll sing on our own,
We'll sing on our own,
We're Aston Villa and we'll sing on our own...

WE'RE GOING TO WIN THE LEAGUE

We're going to win the League,
We're going to win the League,
And now your gonna believe us,
And now your gonna believe us,
We're going to win the League...

WEST BROM AND BIRMINGHAM

F*ck off West Brom,
(and Birmingham),
F*ck off West Brom,
(and Birmingham),
F*ck off West Brom,
(and Birmingham),
F*ck off West Brom,
(and Birmingham)...

WE'VE DONE IT BEFORE WE'LL DO IT AGAIN

We've done it before,
We'll do it again,
We've done it before and we'll do it again.

WHAT DO WE THINK OF BLUES

What do we think of blues?
Shit,
What do we think of shit?
Blues,
Thank you,
Thats alright,
We hate city, we hate city, we hate city,
We hate city, we hate city, we are city haters...

WHAT THE HELL WAS THAT

What the f*ck,
What the f*ck,
What the f*cking hell was that,
What the f*cking hell was that...

WHEN I SEE YOU VILLA

Du, du, du, du, du, du, du,
When I see you Villa,
I go out of my head,
i just can't get enough,
i just can't get enough,
All the things you do to me,
And all the things you said,
i just can't get enough,
i just can't get enough,
We slip and slide as we fall in love,
And I just cant seem to get enough of..
du, du, du, du, du, du.

WHEN I WAS JUST A LITTLE BOY

When I was just a little boy,
I asked my Mother, what should I be,
Should I be Villa should I be Blues,
Here's what she said to me.

Get your father's gun,
And shoot all the City scum,
And support the pride of Brum,
Aston Villa...

WHEN THE VILLA GO MARCHING IN

Oh when the Villa,
(Oh when the Villa),
Go marching in,
(Go marching in),
Oh when the Villa go marching in,
I want to be in that number,
Oh when the Villa go marching in...

WHEN THE VILLA GO LAP-DANCING

Oh when the Villa, go lapdancing,
Oh when the Villa go lapdancing,
I wanna be in that number,
Oh when the Villa go lap dancing...

WHEN YOU'RE SMILING

When you're smiling,
When you're smiling,
The Holte End smiles with you,
When you're laughing,
When you're laughing,
The sun comes shining through,
So stop your crying,
You'll bring on the rain,
So start your smiling,
Be happy again...

WHERE'S YOUR FAMOUS ATMOSPHERE

Where's your famous,
Where's your famous,
Where's your famous atmosphere,
Where's your famous atmosphere?

WHO ARE YA

Who are ya?
Who are ya?
Who are ya?

WHO IS THAT TEAM

Who is that team,
Who plays in yellow and green,
We don't f*****g know,
We don't f*****g,
We don't f*****g know...

...We don't f*****g know,
But what the Villa know,
There f*****g shitttt,
There f*****g shiitttt,
There f*****g s**t.

WHO THE HELL ARE MAN UNITED

Who the f**k are Man Utd,
Who the f**k are Man Utd,
Who the f**k are Man Utd,
When the Villa go marching on on on.

WHO THE HELL ARE YOU

Who the f*ck, who the f*ck,
Who the f*cking 'ell are you,
Who the f*cking 'ell are you,
Who the f*ck, who the f*ck,
Who the f*cking 'ell are you,
Who the f*cking 'ell are you...

WHO'S THAT COPPER

Who's that Copper with the Helmet on,
Dixon, Dixon,
Who's that Copper with the helmet on,
Dixon of Dock Green,
On the beat all day, on the wife all night,
Who's that Copper with the helmet
on............ Dixon of Dock Green!

WHOSE THAT KNOCKING

Whose that knocking on the window,
Whose that knocking on the door,
It's Carson Yeung and his mob selling blues for a Bob,
And they won't beat the Villa anymore.

YACOUBA SYLLA

Sylla, Sylla, Sylla,
He loves the f**king Villa, the Villa, the Villa
Whooooo whooooo whoooo.

YIPPI AYE EH YIPPI AYE OH

Yippi aye eh, yippi aye oh,
Holte Enders in the sky...

YOU ARE MY VILLA

You are my Villa,
My only Villa,
You make me happy when skys are grey,
When skys are grey,
You'll never notice,
How much I love,
So please don't take my Villa away...

YOU KNOW YOU ARE

You're s*it, and you know you are,
You're s*it, and you know you are,
You're s*it, and you know you are,
You're s*it, and you know you are.

YOU SHOULD HAVE STAYED ON THE TELE

Stayed on the tele,
You should have stayed on the tele,
Stayed on the tele,
You should have stayed on the tele...

YOUR SUPPORT

Your support is,
Your support is,
Your support is f***ing s**t.
Your support is f***ing s**t...

YOU'RE CHELSEA'S FEEDER CLUB

You're Chelsea's feeder club,
You're Chelsea's feeder club,
You're Chelsea's feeder club,
You're Chelsea's feeder club...

YOU'RE NOT FIT TO REFEREE

You're not fit,
You're not fit,
You're not fit to referee,
You're not fit to referee.

YOU'RE NOT SINGING ANYMORE

You're not singing,
You're not singing,
You're not singing anymore,
You're not singing anymore.

Printed in Great Britain
by Amazon